CHAPTERS OF THE SOUL

AN ENSEMBLE OF POETIC JOURNEYS

BINEET DWIVEDY

Made with ❤ on the BookLeaf Publishing Platform
www.bookleafpub.in
www.bookleafpub.com

Dedication

"To all readers...
To those who find solace in words, and carry poems in
their heart
To the dreamers who find poetry in the stars,
To the seekers who uncover meaning in silence,
To the lovers who embrace vulnerability as strength—
This collection is for you.
May these words light your path,
As they have illuminated mine."
-BINEET DWIVEDY

Preface

Poetry has always been the language of the soul —a space where emotions find rhythm, thoughts find words, and silence finds voice. This collection is born from moments that lingered longer than others, from emotions that refused to fade, and from stories that demanded to be told.

Each poem in this ensemble is a fragment of a journey, an echo of the heart, or a whisper from the quiet corners of life. Some verses might feel like a soft touch, others like a restless storm, but all are bound by an honest attempt to explore the intricate tapestry of human experience.

This book is for those who seek meaning in fleeting moments, those who find beauty in vulnerability, and those who know that sometimes, a poem says what prose cannot.

It is my hope that as you turn these pages, you will find pieces of yourself reflected in the lines, and that these poems might, in some way, become companions to your own story.

Acknowledgements

This collection would not have been possible without the unwavering support of those who believed in me and my words.

To my family, for fostering my love for language and for standing by me through every step of this journey—your encouragement has been my greatest strength.

To my acquaintances, who lent their ears and hearts to these verses before anyone else— thank you for your honesty, kindness, and inspiration.

To the muses, seen and unseen, who lit the fire of creativity within me—this book is as much yours as it is mine.

Lastly, **to my readers**—your love for poetry keeps the art alive. These poems may have been born from my experiences, but they now belong to you.

1. Chains Broken, Wings Unfurled...

Upon a path both wild and steep,
Through shadows long and whispers deep,
A lone traveller treads, his steps unsure,
Bearing burdens, life bestows so obscure.
The wind, it howls with merciless jeer,
A mirror of doubt, of whispered fear.
Yet forward he moves, though weary and worn, Through
storms unyielding,
Through thickets torn.
Rivers rise, their torrents wide, Symbols of trials life
can't hide.
He builds his bridges, frail yet bold, Over waters murky,
icy, and cold.
Mountains loom with jagged peaks, A climb that tests,
that mocks the weak.
But hand to rock, and heart in fight, He scales the cliffs
in endless night.
The sun he seeks, its gentle gleam, A fleeting hope, a
distant dream.
Yet as he journeys, he comes to find, Strength resides
within the mind.
Each stone, a lesson; each thorn, a test, Shaping the
courage that beats in his chest.

For though alone, he's never bereft— His spirit endures when all else has left.

So on he roams, through dark and light, A beacon of life's grand fight.

The lone traveller, though bent, won't break— For every step, a victory to take.

2. Shadows of a Faded Flame

The sun sinks low, a waning light,
As shadows stretch to claim the night.
A heavy heart, its rhythm slow, Carries the weight of all below.
The echoes of a dream once bright, Now whispers lost in endless night.
The fragile threads of hope unwind, A tangled web, the soul confined.
Winds howl through hollow, empty halls, Where laughter fades, and silence calls.
Each step a burden, every breath, A quiet march toward gentle death.
But in the ashes, embers glow,
A flicker faint, though none may know.
For even in defeat's embrace, A spark may rise, a trace of grace.

3. "I Won't Bow Down.."

When storms arise and darkness reigns,
When life delivers its sharpest pains,
 A heart of steel, unbroken, stands,
With courage forged by its own hands.
The winds may shriek, the seas may roar,
But deep within, there's something more— An ember
bright, a fierce decree: "I shall not bow; I shall stay free."
Each setback whispers, "You are weak,"
 Yet dreams persist, no words they seek.
Through shadows dense, through blinding strife,
Determined steps carve paths to life.
The mountains loom, the climb is steep, But promises
made, the soul must keep.
For every fall births lessons clear,
 And every scar a badge to wear.
So, rise again, defy the night, Harness pain, transform
the fight.
The world may bend, but not the will— A soul
unyielding, unbroken still.

4. Gentle Ripples, Stilled Tides...

A tempest tore through, fierce and wild,
The sky unzipped; the heavens defiled.
Angry winds screamed, trees bent to pray,
Chaos reigned in the heart of the fray.
But now, a hush—the storm is spent,
The world exhales in sweet lament.
Shards of sky, like shattered glass,
Mend themselves as the moments pass.
The earth, a wounded but healing friend,
Wears scars with grace, begins to mend.
Rivers hum, their tears subdued,
Nature whispers in gratitude.
In the silence blooms a quiet song,
Proof that even turmoil won't last long.
The calm, a paragon from ashes reborn,
A gentle embrace after the thorn.

5. Saffron Tide: The Flames Of Freedom

In the heart of the Deccan, where warriors rise,
Echo the sagas beneath open skies.
The Marathas stood, fierce and unbowed,
With courage aflame, like thunder in a cloud.
Through treacherous hills and fortresses steep,
They sowed their legacy for history to keep.
Against the tide of the Mughal might,
They lit the dark with freedom's light.
Shivaji's roar, the lion's decree,
Rang through the land, calling it free.
With sword and shield, they paid the price,
Their blood, the ink of sacrifice.
In every martyr, a flame was born,
A spark of hope for a brighter morn.
They battled storms, they broke the chain,
Their spirits soared, despite the pain.
From Raigad's heights to Sinhagad's wall,
Their tales inspire, their deeds enthrall.
An undying saga, a warrior's creed,
Forever etched in each noble deed.
In their valor, we find our way,
A beacon that shines to this very day.

6. Humility: The Only Might

A man may climb the tallest peak,
His name on lips the nations speak,
Yet if his heart with pride takes flight,
His soul is lost in endless night.
For wealth and power, fleeting, fade,
A transient shadow, swiftly made.
The fame, the glory, shining bright,
Are but a flame consumed by night.
The strongest oak may touch the sky,
 But storms will strike and roots will die.
So too the man who stands alone,
On fragile pride, a kingless throne.
Humble hearts, like rivers deep,
In silence flow, their truths they keep.
They do not boast, they do not claim,
Yet timeless echoes bear their name.
What joy is found in heights of pride,
When love and peace are cast aside?
A gentle soul, a kindly hand,
Are worth far more than titles grand.
The wise will tread the path of grace, No need for gold,
no need for praise.
For in the end, it's love that stays, A quiet light through
darkened days.

So, though the world may tempt and call,
Beware the pride that brings the fall.
A man may own the earth and skies, But humble hearts
alone will rise.

7. Through Fire and Fury: The Champion's Path

In the crucible of trials, you stand,
A force untamed, resolute, grand.
The winds growl fierce, the thunder roars,
Yet your spirit surges, forever soars.
Every stumble, a lesson carved in stone,
Every tear, a seed of strength you've sown.
Through tempests wild, through shadows deep,
Your dreams awaken from their restless sleep.
The whispers of doubt may circle and sneer,
Yet your courage silences every fear.
A heart of fire, a soul so vast,
You rise above the echoes of the past.
The mountains tremble beneath your stride,
The oceans part, the storms subside.
For you are a titan, a force of nature,
A script unwritten, an untold adventure.
Through the labyrinth of life, you carve your way,
A blazing comet in the break of day.
The chains of failure, you shatter and rend,
For your strength knows no limit, no end.
The world may falter, the skies may weep,
But your dreams climb peaks impossibly steep.
Each step you take is a battle won,

Each breath a hymn to the rising sun.
So, march on, warrior, with fire in your eyes,
Conquer the earth, and ascend the skies.
For within your chest burns a radiant light,
 A beacon of hope in the endless night.
Rise, unyielding, embrace your might;
 A champion eternal, a star alight.

8. DIE WITH DUSK: A Shakespearean Sonnet

Lonesome black tears of the sky as lonely as thou in dusk,
doth question thy existence, death so near;
Stormy tiring restrained cries as large as tusk,
Wail for an inch of breath that deport in fear;
Pen down such gigantic feelings terrorizing thy mind,
A contemplation of the task unwritten and undone;
A way to exile from such weirdness to find,
The answer for the safe exit known to none;
Let me live to the fullest ; lamented my heart,
Weep no more, gather glorious moments of dawn to an amazing dusk filled with wonder;
Enough of sorrow to behold thy joy to a new start,
Diverged roads to freedom I chose to be the founder;
The change of nature exhibits the showering of blessings,
When I realized, the soul, a free entity in closed casings.

9. Musings Of The Soul...

In the abyss where shadows cling,
And sorrow weaves its silent string,
 Musings, a heavy shroud,
 Wraps the heart and dims the proud.
Yet within the gloom, a seed does lie,
 A whisper soft beneath the sky.
Hope, a phoenix, faint but true,
Rises bold through ash and rue.
Where tears carve rivers down the face,
Hope paints stars in empty space.
Though despondency binds, a cruel arrest,
Hope presses on, an unyielding guest.
One speaks in echoes, cold and hollow,
 A path of thorns we're forced to follow.
The other hums, a melody sweet,
Calling weary souls to rise, to meet.
For despair may linger, dark and deep,
And lull the heart to restless sleep.
 But hope, unbroken, shines its glow,
A fire that thaws the coldest snow.
Together they dwell, a paradox stark,
 One dims the day, the other sparks.
Yet through this dance, the soul survives,
For hope ensures the spirit thrives.

10. The Hourglass

In a quiet corner, I silently stand,
 An hourglass, shaped by time's own hand.
Trapped within, my sands cascade,
Marking moments, foundations laid.
Each grain, a whisper of journeys past,
Moments fleeting, yet memories cast.
 I neither rush, nor hold them tight,
 I simply flow in endless flight.
"Why cling to the past, or fear the unknown?
 For time, like my sands, cannot be owned.
Cherish now, this fleeting grace,
For the present's beauty is life's embrace."
Though inverted, thrown, or cast aside,
I remain steady, my sands abide.
For trials may tip you, life rearrange,
Yet strength lies in learning to embrace the change.
Oh, traveler, gaze within my glass,
See how moments shift, yet always pass.
For life is but a dance with time,
And fleeting sands are its quiet chime.

11. Whispers Of Silence

Beneath the velvet shroud of dusk,
Silence tiptoes, a ghostly musk.
It drapes itself on weary minds,
A shadowed symphony it binds.
The stars lean close, their voices mute,
As silence strums a trembling lute.
Each note, a void where echoes fade,
 A canvas where no sound is made.
It dances on the windless breeze,
 A phantom waltz through ancient trees.
The leaves—still soldiers, frozen tight,
Salute the monarch of the night.
Silence paints with hues unseen,
 A masterpiece in shades serene.
Its brush, the hush of empty halls,
Its strokes, the tear before it falls.
The heartbeats thrum, a quiet drum,
Each pulse a hymn, both loud and numb.
In silence speaks the loudest truth,
 A bittersweet, eternal youth.
For in the gaps where words desist,
 A galaxy of thoughts exists.
Silence, tender, fierce, and wild,
The universe's voiceless child.

12. Between Silence and Sound

In shadows linger spoken words,
 Fleeting echoes, softly heard.
They dance like ripples in the air,
Unveiling truths, bold and bare.
Yet in the silence whispers keep,
Dreams and sorrows buried deep.
Unspoken phrases weave their thread,
In quiet corners of the head.
The soul, a wanderer lost in time,
Crafts its musings, prose, and rhyme.
It questions stars, it questions night,
 It seeks the warmth of inner light.
Between the said and unsaid lies,
A bridge of yearning, boundless skies.
For words may guide, yet silence molds,
The art of stories untold unfolds.

13. Crossroads Of Destiny

Within his grasp, a pen lies still,
Yet thoughts unchained defy his will.
The silent page, a daunting plea,
Calls him to strive, yet sets him free.
The whispers of the heart grow loud,
Amid the chatter, he's lost, veiled.
Her smile, a fleeting flame,
Distracts his soul, ignites his name.
Books and lessons, a mountain steep,
Dreams and doubts in shadows creep.
The weight of worlds, a future to hold,
Yet here he lingers, caught and bold.
A battle rages, inside his chest,
To rise above, to be his best.
Through storm and calm, he builds his might,
Seeking wisdom, chasing light.
Her gaze, his tether, both bane and bliss,
A gentle pull, an abyss.
But deeper still, a voice within,
Commands him now—it's time to begin.
He steps ahead, not free of scars,
But reaches ever toward the stars.
For though the struggle shapes his pain,
It's the fight that carves his gain. Within his grasp, a pen

lies still,
Yet thoughts unchained defy his will.
The silent page, a daunting plea,
Calls him to strive, yet sets him free.
 The whispers of the heart grow loud,
Amid the chatter, he's lost, veiled.
Her smile, a fleeting flame,
Distracts his soul, ignites his name.
 Books and lessons, a mountain steep,
Dreams and doubts in shadows creep.
The weight of worlds, a future to hold,
Yet here he lingers, caught and bold.
 A battle rages, inside his chest,
To rise above, to be his best.
Through storm and calm, he builds his might,
Seeking wisdom, chasing light.
 Her gaze, his tether, both bane and bliss,
A gentle pull, an abyss.
But deeper still, a voice within,
Commands him now—it's time to begin.
 He steps ahead, not free of scars,
But reaches ever toward the stars.
For though the struggle shapes his pain,
It's the fight that carves his gain.

14. Inseparable: A Shakespearean Sonnet

Adore my love lorn beloved with a cacophony smile,
Cheery blossom with thou appearance,
Doth that create magnitude of feelings awhile,
Landscaping the joyous outburst with fragrance.
Gathering gorgeously the days passed with ease,
Made layers of experiences some bitter, some sweet,
Lovers do need the most of their excitement cease,
Live with the lyrics of love in memories you tweet.
My love is old tinged with mounds of toil,
The longings, the desperations still fresh,
Replaced with dry drum task of life that coil,
Language of love dressed with love and trust that daily I refresh.
Life turned into a beautiful dream to remember,
An inseparable link that occurred in the mornings of September.

15. We, The Sons Of Mother India

Let us sacrifice ourselves at the feet of our mother.
Let us make the soil of our country a crown on our
forehead,
Where the sun always showers its golden rays.
Let every particle of soil sing songs of dedication, let it
tell an immortal tale with the blood of the brave.
The stones of the border are witnesses to our intentions,
Let them always awaken the dreams of the voices of the
people.
We will light lamps even in storms, we will always hoist
the tricolor in the sky.
We are not afraid of storms,
We will not stop in the service of Mother India.
Let us pledge to take the nation to great heights,
Let us pave the way with dedication, courage, and love.

16. Whispers Adrift In The Dreamtide

In the cradle of twilight's tender embrace,
Dreams awaken, dancing through time's haze.
Some, like whispers, find their place,
While others linger, in eyes they blaze.
The ones realized wear a jubilant hue,
 Golden threads woven through the tapestry anew.
They soar, like doves, to the boundless skies,
Singing the tales of the heart's true cries.
Yet some dreams swim, in the depths of sight,
Shimmering quietly, in the veil of night.
Like constellations adrift in an ocean's gaze,
Carrying hope through life's winding maze.
For each dream fulfilled, a spark ignites,
But those unfulfilled lend infinite flights.
They twinkle, a promise of stories untold,
Filling the soul with a courage bold.
So let them linger, those wistful streams,
The realized, the swum—they're all dreams.
Together they weave a life profound,
Where every heartbeat is a sacred sound.

17. A Family's Compass, A Soul's Anchor

In the haven of a family's embrace,
Lies a love that time cannot erase.
 A tapestry woven with threads of care,
Where joys are doubled, and burdens we share.
Mother's touch, gentle as morning dew,
Guides with a heart unwavering and true.
Her whispers soothe, her courage inspires,
Lighting our path through life's fleeting fires.
Father's blessings, steadfast and wise,
 A fortress strong under limitless skies.
His words, a beacon when shadows fall,
His strength, the backbone that carries us all.
Together they stand, a sheltering tree,
Roots deep in love, branches wide and free.
Through every storm, they firmly stay,
Giving us wings to find our own way.
A family's bond, a sacred thread,
Through laughter shared and tears we shed.
Their love, a treasure beyond all measure,
A gift eternal, our life's true treasure.

18. Wings of a Naive Heart

The naive heart beats like a fearless drum,
Singing dreams that have yet to come.
Untouched by fear, unscathed by doubt,
It whispers, "The world is mine to scout."
With wings of hope, it dares to rise,
Chasing the glow of endless skies.
Each cloud a castle, each star a guide,
It journeys far with no one to chide.
Boundless as the horizon's span,
It charts a course where none began.
Through tempest winds and shadowed trails,
It holds steadfast, its passion prevails.
Oh, the naive heart, so raw, so pure,
Its courage vast, its spirit sure.
For in its innocence, there lies the key;
 To dream, to leap, and truly be free.

19. My Past Selves: The Dunes Of Time

I met them on a twilight road,
Faint echoes of the paths I'd strode.
Each self, a fragment, a fleeting shade,
Their voices woven in time's cascade.
The child with eyes wide, dreams unbound,
Wonder clutched in all he found.
He asked me, "What became of hope?
Did you climb each towering slope?"
A rebel youth with fire ablaze,
Daring life with reckless craze.
He scoffed, "Do you still fight the tide,
Or did you learn to run and hide?"
The doubting soul with heavy heart,
Bruised by battles, torn apart.
Her whisper lingered, soft, forlorn,
"Do you feel the weight I've borne?"
And there I stood, their answers held,
In scars I earned, in dreams repelled.
Each questioned mirrored who I'd been,
The struggles lost, the moments win.
"Dear past," I said, my voice, a thread,
"Your echoes shaped the life I've led.
From your fire, I carved my way,

And built the self who stands today."
They smiled, those shades, and turned to fade,
Their truths within me ever stayed.
For every self was part of me,
A chorus in my symphony.
In twilight's glow, I grasped the chain,
Of shattered dreams, and whispered pain.
With each reflection, wisdom grew,
A tapestry stitched from shades of you.
And as I walk this winding course,
I carry forth their silent force.
For every road that I have roamed,
In every heart, I found a home.

20. Beyond the Edge of Tomorrow

Beneath the velvet shroud of dusk,
A lone candle wavers, fighting the musk.
Its golden whispers caress the walls,
As shadows sway in eternal halls.
The trees are sentinels, stoic and tall,
Their whispers etched in the wind's soft drawl.
Leaves pirouette like dancers in flight,
Brushing the edges of encroaching night.
Stars ignite in a canvas of ink,
A symphony of glimmers that dares you to think.
 Each one a story, a fate to unfold,
Echoes of mysteries daringly bold.
A river snakes under the moon's cold gaze,
 Its ripples a language of secretive plays.
Does it lead to a meadow kissed by the sun,
Or a chasm where the brave come undone?
Mountains loom like keepers of lore,
Their faces etched with battles of yore.
Do they cradle kingdoms under their crest,
Or siren songs to test the best?
In this dance where time quietly bends,
The world spins tales with uncertain ends.
Do you stay by the candle's timid flame,

Or chase the stars, untamed, untamed?
The question lingers, hangs in the air,
Like a thread of light, impossibly rare.
What lies beyond? A whisper, a sigh
 Your answer's out there, beneath the sky.

21. Ephemeral Echoes

All good things must draw the curtain,
Like twilight's song, soft and certain.
The petals fade, the rivers wend,
A gentle truth—things come to an end.
Life moves forward, a steady stream,
A patchwork quilt, a fragile dream.
Each moment whispers, fleeting, rare,
A tranquil breath fills the air.
Memories linger, a quiet glow,
Traces of laughter, hearts that know.
Though seasons shift and chapters close,
In every ending, life still grows.
Embrace the stillness, the rare delight,
A flicker of stars in endless night.
For though all good things bid goodbye,
Life goes on—beneath the pains and cry.
Yet in the echoes, treasures gleam,
In shadows cast, we dare to dream.
The laughter shared, the tears we've shed,
A tapestry of words unsaid.
Through all the shifts, the ebb and flow,
Resilience blooms, a constant flow.
With every dusk, a dawn will rise,
Rekindling hopes beneath the skies.

And in the silence, hear the sound,
Of love that lingers, rich and profound.
For every end, a chance to start,
In every journey, the beating heart.

22. To My Beloved...

In the quiet of twilight's gentle fade,
Your shadow lingers where it once played.
A fleeting ghost, a whisper in the air,
A thousand moments, now laid bare.
Each thought of you, a torrent untamed,
A deluge of joy, and a sorrow unnamed.
Laughter echoes in chambers of the past,
Fragile and fleeting, too bright to last.
The scent of rain, the touch of dawn,
Traces of you that were never quite gone.
In every corner, in every hue,
The world remembers, though it's lost you.
I chase the echoes, though they bring pain,
Their weight a comfort, their loss a chain.
For even in absence, you still reside,
An ache in my heart, forever inside.
So I sit, as the memories unfold,
Warming my soul, though the night is cold.
A patchwork of us, though tattered and frayed,
The love remains where the heart once stayed.

23. Raindrops, Like Unspoken Goodbyes

Underneath a canvas of restless grey,
 The raindrops fall, and skies betray
 A storm that brews not in the air,
 But deep within, where wounds lay bare.
They tap upon the window's glass,
 A mournful hymn for love that passed.
 Each drop, a thought that dares to creep,
 A memory lost, a dream in sleep.
Do they carry the weight I bear?
 The ache of longing, the silent despair?
 With every streak upon the pane,
 They mirror my heart, scarred and slain.
The streets glisten, a fractured glow,
 Reflecting fragments of what I know:
 Your laughter, a sunbeam's fleeting touch,
 Your voice, now a whisper I crave too much.
The rain, relentless, pounds the earth,
 As though it seeks to unearth
 The moments we shared, now out of reach,
 Lost treasures scattered along the beach.
And yet, within this storm's embrace,
 I see the trace of your gentle face.
 The wind, it whispers your name aloud,

Among the chaos, beneath the shroud.
Raindrops fall like unspoken goodbyes,
Each one a tear that my soul denies.
They hold the words I could not say,
The love that lingers, though you've gone away.
But storms must pass, as all storms do,
And leave behind a world renewed.
The rain may cease, but its touch remains,
Etched in the soil, in my heart's refrains.
For though you've left, you're never far,
Your memory glows like a distant star.
And as the rain gives way to light,
I hold you close through the endless night.

24. Stitched from Shadows, Rising in Light

My clothes hang tattered, threadbare, torn,
Echoes of battles where hope was worn.
The fabric frays, much like my soul,
Yet I gather the pieces to make me whole.
Each rip, a scar I cannot disguise,
Each tear, a whisper of silent cries.
My heart, shattered, lies in disarray,
Yet I strive to mend it, day by day.
With trembling hands, I weave and sew,
Binding pain where love used to grow.
Patch by patch, I reclaim my name,
Through every stitch, I defy the flame.
My tears are needles, sharp yet true,
Piercing the remnants of what I knew.
Though the seams may strain, though threads may fray,
I refuse to crumble, I find my way.
For strength is born from brokenness,
And courage blooms in emptiness.
I wear my scars like armor strong,
Each tear a verse in my battle song.
Now I stand tall, though storms may call,
With patched-up garments, I bear it all.
For torn clothes and torn emotions fade,

But the spirit endures, undismayed.
So I rise, stitched from pain and fight,
A tapestry woven of shadow and light.
The frays remind me I've come so far,
Every broken thread, now a shining star.

25. Betrayed Yet Unbroken

The path stretches on, jagged and cold,
A story of anguish, of trials untold.
Thorns entwine with each weary tread,
Beneath a sky of shadows overhead.
Each step I take, a burden to bear,
The echoes of treachery hang in the air.
Daggers, unseen, pierce through my soul,
Betrayals' venom has taken its toll.
Once, my heart bloomed in love's gentle glow,
Trust as pure as the untouched snow.
Yet the hand I held, so tender, so near,
Plunged a blade, leaving scars severe.
Fragments of love, scattered like sand,
Slipped through the fingers of a trembling hand.
Dreams once vivid, now pale and torn,
A symphony silenced, a rose de-thorned.
Still, amidst the ruins, I find my fire,
A warrior's spirit that will not tire.
Through countless arrows my body bleeds,
Yet my heart beats strong, fulfilling its needs.
The pain is a melody, haunting yet deep,
A chorus of memories, where sorrow does seep.
But I wield these wounds as a badge of pride,
For even in anguish, I stand, untried.

The world may conspire to see me fall,
 Erect its barriers, erect its walls.
 But mountains yield to the river's flow,
 And I am the tempest that will not bow.
Through forests of grief, through deserts of despair,
 I tread undeterred, unyielding to care.
 I gather my shards, each piece a gift,
 Building a mosaic, letting my spirit lift.
For I am a flame, unquenched by tears,
 A beacon that cuts through the darkest fears.
 Let the path remain dreary, thorny, and wild,
 I stride with the defiance of fate's exiled.
So here I walk, though battered and torn,
 A soul remade, in resilience reborn.
 For life's greatest strength is the power to rise,
 And face the storm with unbroken eyes.

26. Embers of Dawn: A Symphony of Hope

In the cradle of night's somber arms,
A phoenix sleeps, its plumage dimmed,
Ashes spiral like whispered psalms,
Yet beneath lies fire, untrimmed.
Clouds stitched with silver lace unfurl,
Veiling stars with dreams untold,
Dawn tiptoes in on amber pearl,
Breathing life into tales of old.
The river hums in liquid gold,
It carries hymns of earth's embrace,
Each ripple dances, young yet bold,
A timeless waltz, a healing trace.
The oak's gnarled roots clutch ancient pain,
But sapling shoots defy despair,
Leaves murmur songs of sun and rain,
Hope's soft anthem fills the air.
Through ruins choked with ivy's wraith,
A lily blooms with steadfast grin,
Its perfume speaks of boundless faith,
A fragile strength deep within.
Whispers echo where silence stood,
Winds carve hymns through canyon stones,
A symphony of soul and wood,

Resilience found in nature's tones.
Hope awakens—a blazing star,
Rising through shadows' soft decay,
It finds us where our bruises are,
Lighting paths to a brighter day.
In the garden where shadows kneel,
Each heartbeat echoes, soft yet strong,
With roots entwined in time's reveal,
We weave our stories, right the wrong.
The moon, a guardian, watches near,
Casting shadows that cradle dreams,
In every sigh, our doubts and fears,
Transform to rivers, flowing streams.
With every dawn, let courage rise,
A chorus built on dreams reborn,
For in the depths, where longing lies,
The heart, undaunted, greets the morn.

27. Tempest and Granite

Some say a storm reveals the soul,
Its tempests fueled by wrath untamed,
Clouds charged with fury, black as coal,
Lightning strikes, unashamed.
And others see the stone endure,
A stoic face, untouched by fray,
Silent, cold, and resolutely sure,
Its heart unmoved, day by day.
The storm may rage in anger's name,
Its thunder raw, a deafening sound,
Yet stone remains, immune to flame,
Rooted deep in the solid ground.
But storms erode what stone defends,
Time wears away its stubborn pride,
While stone endures, the storm transcends,
Their clash leaves neither satisfied.
For human hearts, both storm and stone,
Conflict shapes us, wild and still,
Passion flares, yet we atone—
Balanced chaos bends to will.

28. Through Chaos, the Star Ascends

Through the veil of misty unknowns,
 Where footsteps falter on shifting sand,
 I forge ahead, though winds have blown,
 Guided by dreams cradled in hand.
The skies may weep, the earth may quake,
 Yet I carry a flame, steadfast and bright,
 Each ember born from trials I take,
 Illuminating shadows of night.
I hear the whispers of ancient trees,
 Their roots entwined in stories deep,
 They sing of courage on every breeze,
 Of promises sown, for me to reap.
I carve a path through jagged stone,
 Each strike a testament of will,
 Through every scar, a truth is shown,
 That mountains yield to purpose still.
My voice may tremble, my heart may strain,
 But my spirit hums a timeless tune,
 Of joy reborn through loss and pain,
 A melody rising with the moon.

29. Where Blood And Earth Converge

When the world grows cold and hearts grow weak,
 When silence stands where words should speak,
 When walls rise tall, brick by bitter brick,
 Our love endures, steadfast and thick.
Oh family, a bond both fragile and strong,
 A place we belong, yet where we go wrong,
 For even when anger ignites the air,
 The roots hold firm, forever there.
You may turn your back, walk far, far away,
 Leave memories scattered in disarray,
 But here I stand, with arms stretched wide,
 A harbor of solace where you can confide.
For love is not a fleeting flame,
 It's not erased by hurt or blame,
 It weathers storms, withstands the frost,
 A compass that guides when we are lost.
I see your pain in the words unsaid,
 The weight you carry, the tears you've shed,
 And though you hide behind shadowed eyes,
 I'll wait in the light where hope never dies.
The rivers may rage, and bridges may burn,
 Yet through the ashes, I'll always return,
 For family's a circle, no start, no end,

A promise unbroken, a hand to lend.
Even when trust falters and cracks appear,
I will be your anchor, steady and near,
For love does not waver, it does not depart,
It's carved into the chambers of my heart.
So if ever you stumble, falter, or fall,
Know I will answer, no matter the call,
For family means rising, again and again,
To heal the wounds, to shoulder the pain.
In moments of doubt, when shadows creep,
I'll guard your secrets, your burdens to keep.
Through laughter and tears, through day and night,
Together we'll find a way to the light.
When whispers echo in the dark of despair,
Remember my heart, it's always laid bare.
For every fracture and every scar,
Can weave us closer, no distance too far.
So take my hand, let's weather the tides,
In this sea of life, where love abides.
For even when paths twist and bend,
We'll find our way home, where worries end.
In the tapestry woven with threads of gold,
Each story we share makes us bold.
And though at times we lose our way,
The ties remain, come what may,
For we are bound by threads unseen,
An eternal bond, pure and keen.

So turn if you must, but know this truth:
Love's roots grow deep, unshaken, uncouth.
And in the end, when the storm has passed,
Family is the shelter that stands steadfast.

30. From Fragments to Wholeness

Once, I stood like a fractured stone,
Weathered by winds, cold and alone,
A restless heart, with shadows sown,
Unsure of my place, my path, my own.
Life was a riddle, harsh and cruel,
A game I played without a rule,
With every fall, I bore the sting,
And questioned what my journey would bring.
I wandered through deserts of despair,
With parched hopes and burdens to bear,
Yet in the distance, faint and true,
A glimmer of love began to break through.
It was family's love, like a gentle flame,
Whispering softly, calling my name,
Their arms outstretched, they held me tight,
Through storms and sorrows, through endless night.
They mended cracks that split my soul,
With warmth and care, they made me whole,
In their embrace, I found my worth,
A steadfast haven on this earth.
And then God's grace, unseen, profound,
Spoke in silence, a sacred sound,
Through every trial, through every tear,

I felt His presence, close and near.
In darkest hours, His light would gleam,
 A quiet hope, a guiding beam,
 He taught me faith, He taught me peace,
 A gift unyielding, love's release.
Life, too, became my greatest muse,
 Its lessons carved, its wisdom infused,
 Through storms that raged and battles fought,
 I gained the strength I once had sought.
Now, I look back at who I was,
 A shadowed figure, tethered because
 I'd yet to learn, I'd yet to see,
 The potential locked inside of me.
Through love, through blessings, through every scar,
 I found the light, I reached the stars,
 The person I am stands rooted, tall,
 A testament to rising after the fall.
So here I stand, with gratitude deep,
 For hands that held and prayers that keep,
 For lessons carved in the heart of strife,
 For family, faith, and the gift of life.